ALEXANDER
HAMILTON

FOUNDING FATHER AND STATESMAN

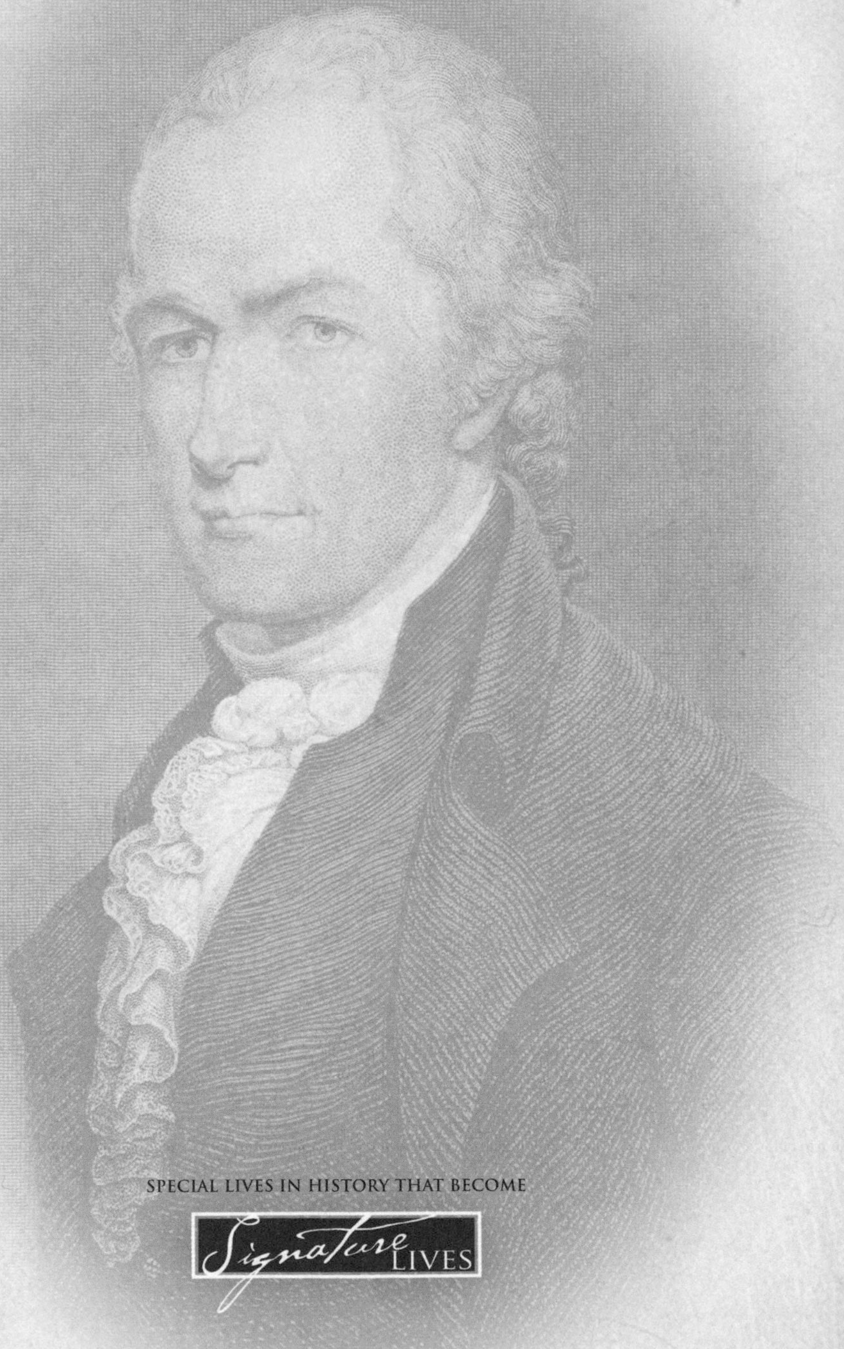

SPECIAL LIVES IN HISTORY THAT BECOME

Signature LIVES

ALEXANDER
HAMILTON

FOUNDING FATHER AND STATESMAN

by Brenda Haugen

Content Adviser: Richard J. Bell,
History Department, Harvard University

Reading Adviser: Rosemary G. Palmer, Ph.D.,
Department of Literacy, College of Education,
Boise State University

COMPASS POINT BOOKS ✺ MINNEAPOLIS, MINNESOTA

Compass Point Books
3722 West 50th Street, #115
Minneapolis, MN 55410

Visit Compass Point Books on the Internet at *www.compasspointbooks.com*
or e-mail your request to *custserv@compasspointbooks.com*

Editor: Heidi Schoof, Sue VanderHook
Lead Designer: Jaime Martens
Photo Researcher: Marcie C. Spence
Page Production: Tom Openshaw, Bobbie Nuytten
Cartographer: XNR Productions, Inc.
Educational Consultant: Diane Smolinski

Managing Editor: Catherine Neitge
Art Director: Keith Griffin
Production Director: Keith McCormick
Creative Director: Terri Foley

Library of Congress Cataloging-in-Publication Data
Haugen, Brenda
   Alexander Hamilton : founding father and statesman / by Brenda Haugen
      p. cm—(Signature lives)
   Includes bibliographical references and index.
   ISBN-13: 978-0-7565-0827-2 (hardcover)
   ISBN-10: 0-7565-0827-4 (hardcover)
   ISBN-13: 978-0-7565-1073-2 (paperback)
   ISBN-10: 0-7565-1073-2 (paperback)
   1. Hamilton, Alexander, 1757-1804—Juvenile literature. 2. Statesmen—
United States—Biography—Juvenile literature. 3. United States—Politics
and government—1783-1809—Juvenile literature. I. Title II. Series.
   E302.6.H2H386 2004
   973.4'092—dc22   2004020898

Signature Lives

REVOLUTIONARY WAR ERA

The American Revolution created heroes—and traitors—who shaped the birth of a new nation: the United States of America. "Taxation without representation" was a serious problem for the American colonies during the late 1700s. Great Britain imposed harsh taxes and didn't give the colonists a voice in their own government. The colonists rebelled and declared their independence from Britain—the war was on.

Table of Contents

1 PLANS FOR THE FUTURE

❧❧❧

One warm summer day in the West Indies, Alexander Hamilton watched his best friend, Edward Stevens, sail off to faraway New York City to begin college. Alexander felt joy for his friend and his new adventure, but he was also sad because he knew he would miss Edward. As Alexander saw the ship disappear in the distance that day in 1769, he probably wondered if he would ever have the chance to take such a trip.

In Alexander's time, a college education was reserved for a wealthy and fortunate few. At that point in his life, Alexander was neither wealthy nor fortunate. He was a 14-year-old orphan with little hope for a bright future. To support himself, Alexander found a job as a clerk. He had just a few

Portrait of Alexander Hamilton by artist
Thomas Hamilton Crawford

Alexander Hamilton was born on the island of Nevis in the Leeward Islands of the West Indies.

years of schooling and no family to turn to for help.

Still, Alexander made ambitious plans for his future. In a letter to Edward at college, he explained that he would not be happy until he had made a success of himself. He wanted no more of "the groveling condition of a clerk or the like, to which my fortune condemns me." Instead, Alexander told his friend, he would be willing to risk his life to get ahead in the world. He knew that others could count on family connections or wealth to help find success. The way Alexander saw it, one way he could make his mark was if there were a war. He believed that war would be his opportunity for glory and success.

Just six years later in 1775, Alexander would earn his chance for glory in the Revolutionary War. As the war progressed, he would become one of General George Washington's most trusted aides and a hero on the battlefield.

Alexander was right about a war providing an opportunity; however, he made his most lasting impact after the war. His intelligence and his dedicated service to General Washington gave him a high position in the newly formed American government. Through his work, he helped to create a strong and lasting system of government for his new country— the United States of America. ℘

2 Hard Times

⋞⋙

Alexander Hamilton grew up where the Atlantic Ocean meets the Caribbean Sea. He was born on January 11, 1755, in the town of Charlestown, on the island of Nevis in the West Indies. But he spent most of his early life in Christiansted, the main city on the nearby island of St. Croix.

St. Croix, an island only 19 miles (30.6 kilometers) long and 5 miles (8 km) across, was one of the wealthiest islands in the West Indies. It played an important role in the triangular trade route that connected Europe, Africa, and the Caribbean in the exchange of slaves, sugar, and rum.

In 1733, the Danish West Indies Company had purchased the island of St. Croix from France and had sent settlers there to form a new colony.

The birthplace of Alexander Hamilton in Charlestown on the island of Nevis, West Indies

After 20 years of company rule, the planters of the three islands of St. Croix, St. Thomas, and St. John had asked the king of Denmark to buy out the company. In 1754, the islands became a royal colony.

The island of St. Croix was originally named Santa Cruz, which means Holy Cross. Explorer Christopher Columbus sailed to the island and named it on his second Caribbean voyage in 1493. It became St. Croix under French rule in the 1600s. Columbus's men went ashore at Salt River Bay, just west of Christiansted. There, they encountered Taino and Carib Indians. This landing was the first recorded encounter between Native Americans and Europeans in the New World.

Most of St. Croix was taken up by large sugar, cotton, and coffee farms called plantations. The plantation owners brought their produce to the city of Christiansted, where it was shipped to markets in North America and other places.

The plantation owners depended on slave labor to grow and harvest their crops. In fact, nearly 90 percent of the people living on St. Croix were slaves. As a boy, Alexander saw slaves being bought and sold on the streets of Christiansted. Many years later, when Alexander was an adult, he would work to free slaves.

Alexander's family life was complicated. Years before Alexander was born, his mother, Rachel Fawcett, had caught the attention of John Michael Lavien, who decided to make her his wife. Although Rachel didn't love John, her mother

forced her to marry him. John had convinced Rachel's mother that he was a wealthy plantation owner, but he was greatly in debt. Rachel was never happy in this marriage, even after the birth of their son Peter.

About four years after Peter's birth, Rachel fell

Danish sugar plantations on St. Croix had wind-driven mills. Many stone ruins remain today.

15 ෬ඁ

in love with James Hamilton, a businessman from Scotland who decided to become a trader in the West Indies. Rachel left her husband and son Peter to go live with James.

Though Rachel was still legally married to John Lavien until 1759, Rachel and James started their own family. James Jr. was born in 1753, and Alexander followed in 1755.

Alexander was an active, healthy boy who loved to play outside. He quickly showed how smart he was when, at only 3 years old, he asked his mother to help him learn to read and write. Because his parents were unmarried, his early years were sometimes difficult. People often looked down on children of unmarried parents and wouldn't associate with them.

When Alexander was about 11 years old, his father James abandoned the family in Christiansted and moved to a nearby island to live by himself. Alexander never saw his father again. His mother was left alone to raise Alexander and his brother James Jr.

To earn money, Rachel opened a store in Christiansted. James Jr. helped support the family by working as a carpenter's apprentice. Alexander took a job as a clerk, keeping records and accounts in a St. Croix trading company owned by Nicholas Cruger. They managed to get by, but tragedy soon

Alexander worked in the counting room of Nicholas Cruger's shipping business.

struck again.

In February 1768, just after Alexander turned 13, he and his mother both came down with tropical fevers. Alexander slowly recovered, but his mother died a few weeks later. She was 39 years old.

Rachel didn't leave much behind for her sons. The little she did have was taken by her oldest son, Peter Lavien. James Jr. and Alexander couldn't count on help from their father, either. In the years since James Hamilton left his family, Alexander had exchanged only a few letters with him. Even after Rachel's death, James offered no financial support or invitation to come to live with his sons.

After Rachel's death, her nephew Peter Lytton

gave her sons a place to live, but the arrangement wouldn't last long. Peter died just one year after Rachel, so the young brothers were left penniless and alone again. With nowhere else to turn, James Jr. went to live with the carpenter he worked for, and Alexander moved in with the Thomas Stevens family. Their son Edward was just a year younger than Alexander, and the two boys soon became best friends.

Other people in the small community of Christiansted stepped forward to help Alexander build a life for himself. Despite his young age, Alexander impressed the town's leaders with his intelligence and hard work.

One of these leaders was Nicholas Cruger, the man Alexander worked for at the trading company. Cruger traded St. Croix's products—mostly sugar, rum, and molasses—for North American goods such as livestock, lumber, and food products. Although Alexander was only a teenager, he played an important role in Cruger's importing and exporting company. When Cruger was away on business, he trusted Alexander to make important decisions

> *Through his work with Nicholas Cruger, Alexander learned to deal with difficult and sometimes dishonest sea captains. He also learned about business, specifically how and when to sell his products. He needed to buy his products at a low price and then sell them at a higher price so he could make a profit and keep the company going.*

New York merchants received shipments of sugar, rum, and molasses from the West Indies.

and give instructions to other workers. In a letter Alexander wrote when he was 16, he scolded one of the company's older ship captains for being late in delivering a shipment.

Alexander also impressed a local minister named Hugh Knox. A collector of books, Knox

owned a large private library. Alexander had only a few years of formal schooling, but he was determined to educate himself. Knox recognized young Alexander's abilities and offered to teach him.

Alexander borrowed books from Knox's library and soon began showing the minister some of the poems he wrote. In 1772, the local newspaper published Alexander's descriptive report of a hurricane that had struck St. Croix.

It began at dusk, at North, and raged very violently 'till ten o'clock. What horror and destruction—it's impossible for me to describe.

In addition to sharing his knowledge and his books with Alexander, Knox shared his moral beliefs with him, too. He taught Alexander to hate slavery, and he warned him about the dangers of drinking too much alcohol. These were lessons Alexander would live by for the rest of his life.

Both Knox and Cruger realized Alexander was bright enough to achieve great things. However, they also knew that if Alexander wanted a successful future, he would need a better education than the St. Croix schools could offer. So the two men, with help from other leaders in the community, arranged for Alexander to go to the American colonies for his education.

In October 1772, 17-year-old Alexander set sail from Christiansted to begin his American education. For Alexander, the 1,500-mile (2,414-km) ocean voyage to Boston, Massachusetts, gave him a chance to put his past behind him and start a new life. ᘒ

3 HAMILTON'S EDUCATION

❧

Alexander Hamilton arrived in Boston about six weeks after he left the West Indies. Immediately, he set out for a city he had heard about from Nicholas Cruger. It was Cruger's hometown—New York City.

Cruger had made arrangements for his business friend, Cornelius Kortright, to help Hamilton get settled. Kortright's business partner had a brother named Hercules Mulligan, and Hamilton would stay with him.

Soon, school started for Hamilton. His few years of schooling under Hugh Knox in St. Croix were not enough preparation to qualify for college classes. So Knox arranged for Hamilton to enroll in an academy in Elizabethtown, New Jersey. The plan was for Hamilton to take classes there for several years

The Brooklyn Ferry carried passengers across the East River from New York to Long Island in the 1700s.

before moving on to college. Knox had attended the College of New Jersey (now called Princeton University), and he wanted Hamilton to go there, too. Hamilton had his own plan, though. As ambitious as ever, he set his mind on advancing quickly through his pre-college studies.

Francis Barber (1751-1783), Hamilton's teacher, later became an officer in the Continental Army.

The academy in Elizabethtown proved to be the perfect place for Hamilton to learn. His teacher was Francis Barber, a Princeton graduate who was only about four years older than Hamilton. Barber let his students work independently and at their own speed.

Hamilton put in very long days. He studied late into the night and rose early in the morning to continue studying. In order to enter college, Hamilton needed to learn Latin and Greek. He also studied French and worked on his math skills. By spending all of his free time studying, Hamilton finished several years of studies in less than one year.

His goal now was to finish his college work just as quickly. He told the officers of the College of New Jersey that he wanted to move through his studies at his own fast pace. They told Hamilton he could not make his own schedule for college study at their school, so he decided to go to a school that would let him follow his own plan. He enrolled at King's College (now Columbia University) in New York City in 1773.

Hamilton studied at King's College for more than two years, but he never graduated. His studies were interrupted by the American Revolution. His boyhood prediction that a war would provide him with an opportunity for success was about to come true.

> *The first thing his new classmates noticed about Alexander was his unique way of studying. He liked to read books as he walked. Often he could be found talking to himself—reading sentences over and over in order to memorize them.*

When Hamilton arrived in New York from the West Indies in 1772, the relationship between Great Britain and her American colonies was already strained. Many Americans objected to the new taxes that Great Britain had imposed on the colonies. They claimed that the British government had no right to tax the colonies as long as the colonies had no say in that government. "No taxation without representation" became one of the rallying cries of American patriots who were strong supporters of the colonies.

In 1774, each of the colonies sent representatives to Philadelphia, Pennsylvania, for a Continental Congress. This Congress vowed to resist British taxes, but not all American colonists agreed with that position. Those Americans who supported the

Colonists in New York marched in protest of the Stamp Act of 1765. They continued to express their disapproval for more than 10 years.

British government's policies were called loyalists.

While still a student at King's College, Hamilton decided to take the side of the patriots. In 1774 and 1775, he published essays defending the actions of the Continental Congress. Hamilton wrote that if the colonies continued to pay taxes without being represented in the British government, they would be no better than slaves. Hamilton did not put his name on his essays, signing them only "A Friend to America."

In Boston, New York, and other cities, people took to the streets to protest British taxes on the American colonies. Sometimes those protests turned violent, and British officials were attacked. In response, the British government sent more military troops to the colonies to get things under control.

In coffeehouses and other meeting places where people gathered to talk politics, Hamilton's essays created a great deal of discussion. People argued about who might have written such brilliant essays. Their guesses included some of the best-known political leaders of the day. No one guessed that the author was actually a young man from a small island in the West Indies. But soon, everyone would know Hamilton's name.

4 AT WAR

❦

British soldiers stationed in Boston, Massachusetts, heard that rebellious colonists were storing guns and other weapons in the nearby town of Concord. On April 19, 1775, British soldiers attempted to seize the weapons in Concord. However, they were met by an armed colonial militia in Lexington, and shots were fired. The Revolutionary War had begun.

The shot fired at Concord became known as "the shot heard round the world" because it was an event with worldwide significance. It signaled the start of the war between Britain and its North American colonies, and it also inspired people from other countries to stand up to unfair governments.

With the start of the war, Hamilton had the chance to do more than write for the patriot cause.

Minutemen, who were soldiers ready to fight in a minute's notice, fought British toops in the Battle of Lexington.

Colonial militias were
made up of volunteers
of all ages and from
all walks of life.
Farmers, merchants,
students, and sailors
joined together in the
fight for freedom.
Some militias later
became part of the
Continental Army
under the command
of General George
Washington. Others
kept their own leaders
throughout the war and
fought bravely alongside
Continental soldiers.

In 1775, he joined a militia preparing to defend New York against the British. Hamilton's volunteer company wore green coats and leather hats with the words "Liberty or Death" written across the front. The group practiced its drills every morning in a New York City churchyard not far from King's College.

Though he knew his education was important, Hamilton decided to quit college. He believed the patriot cause was more important than earning a college degree.

On March 14, 1776, 21-year-old Hamilton was made a captain in the Continental Army, the military force formed by the colonies. A captain had command of his own artillery company. One soldier described Hamilton as he led his company:

I noticed a youth, a mere stripling, small, slender, almost delicate in frame, marching beside a piece of artillery with a cocked hat pulled down over his eyes.

Hamilton joined the Continental Army during

one of its most trying times. As the war raged, the army was defeated in battle after battle by British troops. Each day more soldiers deserted the army and went home. General George Washington struggled to keep soldiers from leaving. At the end of 1776 and into early 1777, however, Washington's troops won two important battles. Alexander

Alexander Hamilton was a weapons officer in the Continental Army.

Washington Crossing the Delaware, *by German-born American painter Emanuel Gottlieb Leutze*

Hamilton took part in both of them.

First, Washington launched a Christmas night surprise attack to win the Battle of Trenton, New Jersey. Washington's troops had crossed the Delaware River under the cover of darkness. Then, Hamilton's artillery unit marched 12 miles (19.3 km) through a nighttime snowstorm to reach Trenton. In the morning, they were part of the group of soldiers that launched the successful attack on the unsuspecting enemy troops.

A week later, in early January, Hamilton was

involved in another American victory, the Battle of Princeton. Hoping to surprise the enemy again, Hamilton ordered his men to make as little noise as possible as they advanced toward the British position in Princeton, New Jersey. To muffle the sound of their cannon wheels rolling on the ground, they wrapped them in rags.

Washington and his troops surrounded British troops, who had taken cover in the main building of the College of New Jersey. Hamilton's men opened fire with their cannons. Trapped in the building and under fire, the British quickly surrendered. Marching at the head of his troops, Hamilton finally marched into the College of New Jersey—the same college that had turned down his application just a few years earlier.

During the two battles, General Washington witnessed Hamilton's quick thinking and his bravery under fire. The general needed officers to help him run the Continental Army. He needed soldiers who "can think for me as well as execute orders," Washington explained. "If they can write a good letter, write quick, are methodical and diligent, it is all I expect to find in my aides." Hamilton was the perfect person for the job. In 1777, Hamilton

Members of General George Washington's personal staff were a close-knit group. They called themselves "the family."

joined Washington's personal staff as an aide and was promoted from captain to the rank of lieutenant colonel.

George Washington was one of the most well-known and much-loved Americans of his day. He was a patient man who handled pressure well. On the other hand, Hamilton, only 22 years old, was eager to make a name for himself. Full of pride, Hamilton sometimes acted rashly and spoke before thinking of the consequences. Despite their differences, Washington and Hamilton worked well together and became lifelong friends.

As an aide, Hamilton prepared reports for Washington. Information in the reports was gathered from people living in areas occupied by the British, from British deserters, and from released prisoners of war. The reports gave Washington an idea of what the British military was planning for future attacks.

However, Hamilton's biggest job was writing letters for Washington. Hamilton wrote letters to generals, Congress, and state officials. Even if Washington didn't give him much direction about what to say, Hamilton seemed to know what Washington

Although working with General Washington kept him busy, Hamilton still found time to write long essays calling for changes in the American government. He was particularly concerned about how finances and taxes were being handled in the new country.

Hamilton served five years as George Washington's chief of staff. He was appointed the first of 32 aides-de-camp, or personal assistants, to the general.

wanted to express. Hamilton's writing skills became even more important when France joined the United States as an ally to help in the war against the British. Because he could speak and write French, Hamilton was able to write letters for Washington to French officers in their own language.

35

Written in 1781, the Articles of Confederation was the agreement that combined the original 13 states under one federal government. In creating the Articles of Confederation, American leaders tried to balance the rights of the states with the need for a national government. The Articles allowed Congress to declare war, negotiate peace, establish an army and navy, issue and borrow money, and establish relations with other countries. The Articles did not allow Congress to levy taxes, regulate trade, or make decisions for the states.

As Washington's aide, Hamilton learned a lot about how the new country's government worked. He came to the conclusion that a major problem with the new federal government system was that it lacked the power to get important things done for the nation as a whole. Under the Articles of Confederation that joined the states together, most of the power belonged to the individual state governments. Getting the 13 states to agree on vital issues and work together was nearly impossible.

The federal government did not have the authority to raise money through taxes but instead had to ask the states for money. Hamilton saw this was going to cause major problems. Often the states said no. As a result, the federal government didn't have enough money to feed or supply the army during much of the war. Hamilton came to believe that if the United States were to survive, it needed a government with authority to solve problems. Why couldn't the rest of the country understand this?

As Washington's aide, Hamilton came in contact with many leaders of the American Revolution. He became friends with some of the most prominent political figures in the United States. Despite his

Major battles of the Revolution were fought throughout the colonies.

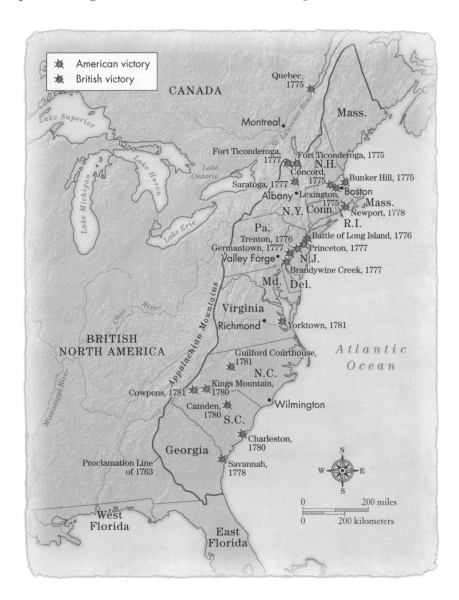

young age and limited experience in politics, Hamilton didn't hesitate to share his ideas for the new country with them. He not only wanted to further his own political career, he also truly believed he had valuable opinions to share.

As charming as he was hard working, Hamilton also enjoyed a lively social life. Women often showed up at army headquarters, where social events and dances were held. Hamilton was quite popular with the young ladies. He was a good dancer and was considered rather good looking. Only 5 feet 7 inches (1.7 meters) tall, Hamilton appeared taller because he stood so straight and looked so dignified. His hair was brown with a hint of red, and his rosy cheeks went well with his light skin. Perhaps his most striking feature was his eyes, so deep blue they almost appeared violet.

Elizabeth Schuyler's father, Philip Schuyler, was named a New York delegate to the Continental Congress at the beginning of the Revolutionary War. In addition, he served as a major general in the Continental Army. Once the war ended and the Constitution was ratified, Schuyler served as one of New York's first senators.

At one of these social events, Hamilton met Elizabeth Schuyler. Elizabeth was the daughter of Philip Schuyler, a powerful New York politician and landowner who was visiting General Washington. Hamilton was dazzled by what he called Elizabeth's "beauties, virtues and graces."

Elizabeth—or Betsy, as Hamilton called her—was tiny, sweet-tempered, and shy. Hamilton fell in love with her almost instantly.

Alexander and Elizabeth were married on December 14, 1780, in the Schuyler mansion in Albany, New York. In addition to the important contacts that Hamilton made through his job, his mar-

Elizabeth Schuyler Hamilton was often called Betsy or Eliza.

riage now brought him into regular contact with the wealthy and powerful.

Though he was now happily married, Hamilton was growing tired of his job at General Washington's headquarters. He wanted to lead troops in battle, not spend his time writing letters to Congress. His new father-in-law urged him to reconsider. Why risk his life in battle when he already was helping the patriot cause? Hamilton patiently listened and then ignored the advice. He quit his job as Washington's aide and set out to find a battlefield command in the army.

Hamilton's timing was excellent. By 1781, with the help of the French army and navy, American troops had trapped a British army at Yorktown, Virginia. Hamilton was given the command of a battalion that would take part in the attack on the British troops. It was his job to capture a small but important British fort that blocked the way to Yorktown. The fort was protected by ditches and barricades made of logs sharpened at the top to injure attackers. British cannons and marksmen were stationed inside the fort.

On the night of October 14, Hamilton led his troops in the attack. Advancing through the darkness with their bayonets ready, they swarmed over the barricade. After a brief fight, Hamilton and his men took the British troops prisoner. In an official

army report, Hamilton was complimented for his well-known talents and gallantry in leading the attack. Now the Continental Army was in control of the path to Yorktown. The British were trapped between the Continental Army and a French fleet just off the Virginia coast.

Just five days later, on October 19, 1781, the British at Yorktown surrendered. The victory gave independence to the new United States of America. ✑

At Yorktown, Virginia, Hamilton showed great bravery by personally leading a bayonet charge on Redoubt #10, an important British stronghold.

5 AFTER THE REVOLUTION

Chapter

❦

After serving at Yorktown, Hamilton rushed home to New York to begin a new life with his wife Elizabeth. They welcomed their first son Philip into the world on January 22, 1782. Hamilton called the baby "a very fine gentleman, the most agreeable in his conversation and manners of any I know."

That same year, Hamilton took the examination to become a lawyer in the state of New York. Always a devoted student, Hamilton taught himself what he needed to know. While some people spent years studying to become lawyers, it took Hamilton six months to master the law. He studied nearly every waking moment of the day and passed the exam. In July, he was admitted to the New York bar, a term for those who have the qualifications to be a lawyer.

Alexander Hamilton was a self-made man, who worked hard to create a better life for himself.

Robert Morris, a merchant and banker from Pennsylvania, was one of six people to sign both the Declaration of Independence and the Constitution. Because he raised large amounts of money for the Continental Army during the Revolutionary War, Morris became known as "the financier of the American Revolution."

On July 2, 1782, Superintendent of Finance Robert Morris appointed Hamilton to a new post—receiver of continental taxes for New York. His job involved collecting money voluntarily given by the state to help support the nation's government. Hamilton was not very excited about his new job. It was difficult, and it didn't pay very well. New York, like several other states, really did not want to provide money to fund the national government. Many states saw themselves as independent countries, with the national government being more of a foreign power like Great Britain. In a letter to Morris, Hamilton called the system of taxation "radically vicious" and "unproductive to the Government. . . . There seems little for a Continental Receiver to do," he wrote in frustration.

Hamilton spent five months as the continental receiver and hated every minute of it. This experience further strengthened his belief that the federal government would need more power to tax its citizens, if the new country were going to succeed.

The same theme came up again and again in Hamilton's work. In July 1782, he was elected by the

New York State Legislature to serve as a delegate to the Second Continental Congress. At the time, the biggest problem facing the Continental Congress was how to pay the nation's growing debt. The new U.S. government owed enormous sums of money to businesses, individuals, and foreign governments for loans they had given the young country after the end of the war. One way to pay the debt would be to raise money through new taxes. However, Congress could not impose taxes without the unanimous agreement of all the individual states. As Hamilton had already learned, the 13 states rarely agreed.

John Adams, Gouverneur Morris, Alexander Hamilton, and Thomas Jefferson were leading members of the Continental Congress.

It was obvious to Hamilton that the nation would need a better way to raise money. Without the power

to tax at a national level, he believed the United States would never be a powerful nation. "We must secure our union on solid foundations," Hamilton wrote to a friend.

Yet many states still feared giving the federal government too much power. They had so recently escaped British tyranny that they were afraid of trading one tyrant for a new one. While their fears were understandable, Hamilton believed that a weak federal government could be just as dangerous as a powerful one. But most people weren't ready to accept that argument.

The new nation still was dealing with other problems left over from the Revolutionary War. There were many legal disputes about who owned what and how to deal with property that was taken over during the war. As a lawyer, Hamilton became involved in these disputes.

When the British finally left New York in November 1783, Hamilton opened a law office on Wall Street in New York City. Although he considered himself a patriot, he found himself defending many loyalists during his first years as a lawyer. Even though the loyalists had continued to support the king of England during the war, Hamilton still felt they had rights in the new country.

In one case, he defended a British businessman, Joshua Waddington, who was being sued by a New

York City woman named Elizabeth Rutgers. Rutgers had owned and operated a brewery in New York before the British took over the city in September 1776. Rutgers, a patriot, was forced to flee, leaving her brewery unattended. During that time, the British military ran it and then allowed Waddington to take over. When the war ended, Rutgers wanted her brewery back and wanted to be paid for the time that both the British and Waddington had used it.

When the British left New York City in 1783, after seven years of occupation, George Washington and the Continental Army rode through the streets in celebration.

After the war, New York State had passed a law called the Trespass Act. It was designed to help colonists sue the loyalists for use of their businesses and homes during the war. However, as part of the peace treaty with Great Britain, the United States had agreed to throw out all claims for damages caused by the war. Hamilton found himself in another battle between the power of the states and the federal government.

The case went before the New York City Mayor's Court in the summer of 1784. In time, the argument Hamilton used in this case became one of the cornerstones of the U.S. Constitution. States could not pass laws that violated national laws. During the case, the lawyers for Rutgers pointed out that this was not yet true. New York did not have to go along with what Congress had agreed to in a treaty, they argued. They warned the court that it didn't have the power to overturn New York's Trespass Act.

While the court may have agreed with Hamilton, it tried to compromise. The decision made no one happy. On August 27, 1784, Mayor James Duane, who served as judge, awarded Rutgers damages for part of the time Waddington ran the brewery. Duane added that he wouldn't overturn the Trespass Act because the court did not have that power over the legislature.

In the early 1780s, Hamilton opened the first bank in New York City. The Bank of New York was funded by a group of wealthy local businessmen. Two years later, its stock became the first corporate stock traded on the New York Stock exchange.

To Hamilton's disappointment, the Trespass Act continued to be enforced in New York, but

Alexander Hamilton argued in court for a stronger national government.

he continued to fight it in the state assembly and in the newspapers. In anonymous letters to the editor, Hamilton said the nation's peace treaty needed to be followed. He also said he believed loyalists needed to be treated fairly in order for the nation to heal. Although Hamilton didn't sign the letters with his name, people in the community knew he had written them. By the end of the decade, partly because of Hamilton's efforts, the Trespass Act and other laws that took away rights from loyalists were overturned. ᴥ

6 THE CONSTITUTIONAL CONVENTION

Chapter

ornamental divider

On January 12, 1787, Hamilton took a seat in the New York State Assembly. He was popular among merchants and manufacturers, and he also gained support through his influential father-in-law, Philip Schuyler.

That same year, Hamilton joined a group of representatives from several states who gathered in Annapolis, Maryland. They met to discuss whether changes should be made to the Articles of Confederation. Hamilton argued for a new plan of government. At this meeting, plans were made for a Constitutional Convention to be held that year in Philadelphia, Pennsylvania. Hamilton wrote the report of this conference and submitted it to Congress.

The Constitutional Convention met at the State House, now called Independence Hall, in Philadelphia, Pennsylvania.

Even as plans were being made for the convention, new crises faced the United States. Because of the weakness of the new federal government, people were reluctant to place much value in American paper money. Hard times gripped much of the young nation. Massachusetts farmers led a violent uprising against state taxes. Riots and protests followed in several other states. The U.S. government seemed to be in danger of financial failure.

Hamilton was chosen as one of the delegates from New York to attend the Constitutional

Benjamin Franklin, Alexander Hamilton, and others discussed the framing of the Constitution in Philadelphia.

Convention in Philadelphia. Not only was he pleased to be a delegate, he was glad New York decided to participate at all. The New York Assembly didn't support the Continental Congress's request to levy import duties, which were taxes on goods coming into the country. Yet Hamilton knew the country needed some way to collect money in order to keep running.

Like Alexander Hamilton, Edmund Randolph had briefly served as an aide to General George Washington during the Revolutionary War. In 1789, Randolph was appointed by President Washington to serve as the first United States attorney general.

Hamilton's ideas contradicted those of his fellow New York delegates, Robert Yates and John Lansing. While Hamilton was a nationalist in favor of a strong federal government, Yates and Lansing favored strong states with a weak federal government. Regardless, Hamilton listened quietly as others presented their plans during the first month of the convention.

The Virginia Plan, presented to the convention May 29, 1787, by Virginia delegate Edmund Randolph, was favored by the states with larger populations. This plan provided for three branches of national government—executive, judiciary, and legislative. The legislative branch would be broken into two groups, with representation in each group determined by a state's population. This meant that states

George Washington, known for his patience and fairness, was chosen to lead the Constitutional Convention.

with many people would get more representatives than states with fewer people.

Another plan, called the New Jersey Plan, was favored by the smaller states. Presented by New Jersey delegate William Patterson, this plan called for the same three branches of government. However, the legislative branch would include just one group, and each state would have an equal number of representatives. The New Jersey Plan also gave the new legislative branch the power to tax and regulate trade.

Hamilton believed nei-
ther plan was strong
enough. On June 18,
1787, a hot, steamy
Monday, Hamilton
spoke to the dele-
gates for several
hours. He proposed
a fairly radical plan
that, he hoped, would
result in a moderate
compromise. Hamilton
exaggerated his ideas so that
even if the delegates agreed with only
some of them, he would feel his speech was successful.

Hamilton pushed for a strong central government
with enough power to make the country secure and
financially stable. He suggested that senators and a
president be elected to serve for the rest of their lives.
He recommended that state governors should be
appointed to lifelong terms by the president, and he
leaned toward abolishing state governments entirely.
He also wanted the president to have the power to
totally kill a legislative bill with a presidential veto.

To many, Hamilton appeared to be proposing a
government that seemed very much like the British
monarchy. The war against Great Britain had been

*Alexander
Hamilton's
speech at the
Constitutional
Convention in 1787
lasted five hours,
the longest speech
of the convention.*

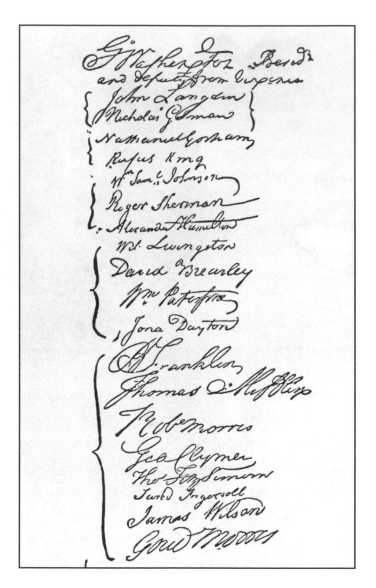

The signatures of some of the leading members of the Constitutional Convention

over less than six years and was still fresh in the minds of the delegates. It is no surprise that Hamilton's bold plan was rejected.

Yates and Lansing, the other New York delegates, left the convention after six weeks because they were opposed to a strong central government. This left New York without official representation. Since Hamilton would not be allowed to cast votes on any issues alone, he too left the convention on June 30, 1787.

George Washington, who represented Virginia at the convention, was disappointed. He wrote Hamilton a letter on July 19, saying, "I am sorry you went away. I wish you were back." Washington got his wish. On August 13, Hamilton returned to help finish up the convention's work.

After a long debate and compromises on the most difficult issues, the convention produced a new constitution for the United States. The delegates signed the document on September 17, 1787, but it would take effect only if it was ratified, or approved, by at least nine of the 13 individual states. It would prove to be a tough battle. ℘

We the People

of the United States, in order to form a more perfect Union, establish Justice, insure domestic Tranquility, provide for the common defence, promote the general Welfare, and secure the Blessings of Liberty to ourselves and our Posterity, do ordain and establish this Constitution for the United States of America.

Article. I.

Article. II.

Article. III.

Article. IV.

Article V.

Article VI.

Article. VII.

done

in Convention by the Unanimous Consent of the States present the Seventeenth Day of September in the Year of our Lord one thousand seven hundred and Eighty seven and of the Independance of the United States of America the Twelfth. In Witness whereof We have hereunto subscribed our Names.

attest William Jackson Secretary

G⁰. Washington—Presidt. and deputy from Virginia

Delaware
Geo: Read
Gunning Bedford jun
John Dickinson
Richard Bassett
Jaco: Broom

Maryland
James McHenry
Dan of St Thos. Jenifer
Danl Carroll

Virginia
John Blair—
James Madison Jr.

North Carolina
Wm. Blount
Richd. Dobbs Spaight.
Hu Williamson

South Carolina
J. Rutledge
Charles Cotesworth Pinckney
Charles Pinckney
Pierce Butler

Georgia
William Few
Abr Baldwin

New Hampshire
John Langdon
Nicholas Gilman

Massachusetts
Nathaniel Gorham
Rufus King

Connecticut
Wm. Saml. Johnson
Roger Sherman

New York
Alexander Hamilton

New Jersey
Wil: Livingston
David Brearley
Wm. Paterson
Jona: Dayton

Pennsylvania
B Franklin
Thomas Mifflin
Robt Morris
Geo. Clymer
Thos. FitzSimons
Jared Ingersoll
James Wilson
Gouv Morris

Chapter

7 WORKING FOR RATIFICATION

⚬⚬⚬⚬⚬

When the Constitutional Convention closed, Alexander Hamilton immediately turned his attention to the fight for ratification of the new Constitution. He worked on a series of newspaper articles that explained why the Constitution should be supported. He teamed up with James Madison and John Jay to write 85 articles urging ratification. Although most of the articles were written by Hamilton, they were signed "Publius"—after a hero of ancient Rome. Together, the articles form a book known as *The Federalist*.

On December 7, 1787, Delaware became the first state to ratify the Constitution. Other states soon followed. New Hampshire was the ninth state to vote for ratification, and the new Constitution took effect

Alexander Hamilton worked for ratification of the U.S. Constitution, approved on June 21, 1788.

on June 21, 1788.

But the large states of New York and Virginia had not yet approved the document. Their approval was needed to ensure the new Constitution's success. The discussion was especially fierce in Hamilton's home state of New York.

In April 1788, New York voters went to the polls to choose delegates to attend a state ratifying convention in June. Most of the delegates chosen were people who were against a strong federal, or central, government. They were called Anti-Federalists. Hamilton and other delegates in favor of a strong federal government, or Federalists, would have to work hard to get the Anti-Federalists to change their minds and support the Constitution.

New York Governor George Clinton, Robert Yates, and others spoke out publicly against the Constitution. Hamilton spoke again and again before the New York state convention, trying to convince the leaders to ratify the Constitution.

Eventually, the opposition softened—partly out of fear.

At one point, Anti-Federalists from New York asked for certain amendments to the U.S. Constitution. They would approve the Constitution on one condition: they could withdraw that approval if their amendments weren't made. When Congress rejected their request, they backed down and approved the Constitution, but they still asked that the amendments be considered.

Title page of The Federalist, *1877*

THE

FEDERALIST:

ADDRESSED TO THE

PEOPLE OF THE STATE OF NEW-YORK.

NUMBER I.

Introduction.

AFTER an unequivocal experience of the ineffi-cacy of the subsisting federal government, you are called upon to deliberate on a new constitution for the United States of America. The subject speaks its own importance; comprehending in its consequences, nothing less than the existence of the UNION, the safety and welfare of the parts of which it is com-posed, the fate of an empire, in many respects, the most interesting in the world. It has been frequently remarked, that it seems to have been reserved to the people of this country, by their conduct and example, to decide the important question, whether societies of men are really capable or not, of establishing good government from reflection and choice, or whether they are forever destined to depend, for their political constitutions, on accident and force. If there be any truth in the remark, the crisis, at which we are arrived, may with propriety be regarded as the æra in which

A   that

While the New York ratifying convention met, New Hampshire became the ninth state to approve the Constitution, making it the law of the land. If New

York and other states still debating ratification did not support the U.S. Constitution, would they become separate little nations of their own? Would they be isolated and cut off from trade with states that did support the Constitution? Anti-Federalists arguing against ratification became worried about the consequences of not signing the Constitution.

Knowing the Constitution had been approved in more than nine states and that New York likely would follow, Constitution supporters staged a parade down the streets of New York City on July 23, 1788. Banners, floats, and jubilant citizens celebrated on the streets of Broadway, Great Dock, and Queen.

The ship of state parade on Wall Street honored Alexander Hamilton and the new U.S. Constitution.

Tradesmen and important businessmen also marched in the parade, including Hamilton's former boss Nicholas Cruger.

At the head of the parade was a model of a sailing ship that appeared to float "with flowing sheets and full sails down Broadway." The ship, named *The Hamilton* in honor of Alexander Hamilton, was manned by 30 people and pulled by 10 horses. At 10:00 A.M., 13 guns—one for each state in the Union—fired from *The Hamilton* to signal the start of the grand celebration.

Three days later, on July 26, 1788, the delegates to the New York ratifying convention approved the Constitution with a 30-27 vote. Virginia had also approved it on July 2. Finally, the country could become truly united. ✍

> The Hamilton *was built by New York City shipyard workers and carpenters. Though they had to build it very quickly, workers created all the details of a real ship.*

8 IN WASHINGTON'S CABINET

⚬∽⚬

The new U.S. Constitution called for a president to lead the United States. There was no question about who would be the first president. There was only one candidate—George Washington. He was elected without opposition.

On April 30, 1789, Alexander Hamilton joined the crowd that watched Washington take the oath of office at Federal Hall in New York City, the new nation's temporary capital.

One of Washington's first tasks was to select the members of his Cabinet—the heads of the various executive departments. Hamilton hoped Washington would remember his days as an aide during the war and call upon him to help with the new government. Hamilton wasn't disappointed.

George Washington was inaugurated as the first president of the United States on April 30, 1789.

Washington and his Cabinet: Henry Knox, secretary of war; Alexander Hamilton, secretary of the treasury (standing); Thomas Jefferson, secretary of state; and Edmund Randolph, attorney general.

In early September, the U.S. Treasury Department was created to deal with the country's finances. Washington selected Alexander Hamilton as the first secretary of the treasury. His job was to build a firm financial foundation for the new nation. This difficult task included finding a way to pay the country's debts and to establish its credibility with other nations.

Hamilton knew he needed to hire experienced people to help him. Within months, the Treasury Department included about 30 clerks in its New York headquarters. In addition, collectors and surveyors worked throughout the new nation to collect taxes that would fund the government's work.

One of the first ideas Hamilton proposed as secretary of the treasury was a plan to raise money through a system of tariffs, or taxes, on goods shipped in or out of the country. The tariffs would help the federal government pay off the nation's war debts and the debts of individual states, as well.

At the time, Hamilton calculated the nation's debt to foreign countries at $11.7 million, and the debt within its borders at $44.4 million. The debts of the individual states totaled $25 million. While the total debt seemed like a lot, it only amounted to about $20 for each of the 4 million Americans. Hamilton predicted the new nation could pay the debt fairly quickly.

Some members of Congress criticized Hamilton's plan for the federal government to take over the payment of state debts. States such as Virginia had already paid off their own debts. Virginia's leaders didn't think it was fair that the federal government should pay the debts of other states when Virginia had taken care of itself.

On June 2, 1790, the U.S. House of Representatives passed

Virginia wasn't alone in thinking it unfair that the federal government pay off debts for the states. Maryland and Georgia had paid off much of their debts. On the other hand, Massachusetts, Connecticut, and South Carolina had large debts and were thrilled with Hamilton's plan. The remaining states stood somewhere in the middle.

One of the biggest
issues for the new
country was choosing
a site for the capital.
In the Compromise of
1790, Philadelphia was
chosen as the capital
for 10 years. After that,
the capital would
move to a site on
the Potomac River.
Supporters of the
Philadelphia site
went along with the
compromise because
they believed once
the capital moved to
Philadelphia, it would
never be moved again.
They were wrong.

Hamilton's funding bill, but it did not include the state debt payment section. The bill then went on to the U.S. Senate, where the senators changed the bill back to include assumption of state debts. The two houses of Congress couldn't reach an agreement.

Working with Secretary of State Thomas Jefferson of Virginia, Hamilton agreed to a compromise. Virginia's leaders agreed to support Hamilton's plan if he supported a plan to move the nation's capital out of New York City and build it on the banks of Virginia's Potomac River. Both houses of Congress approved this compromise, and 10 years later, the city of Washington, D.C., on the Potomac River became the nation's capital, the only U.S. city that is not part of a state.

Another controversial idea that Hamilton suggested was to create a national bank modeled after the Bank of England. Hamilton claimed that the bank would help American businesses grow and allow the government to borrow money when it needed it. Others said that Hamilton's national bank would only help bankers in big cities and hurt farmers in the southern states. Some also said the Constitution didn't give the government the power to set up a bank. George Washington, however, believed that Hamilton's bank would help the United States. He signed the Bank of the United States into existence in 1791. This bank eventually grew into what is now called the Federal Reserve System.

The First Bank of the United States, founded by Alexander Hamilton in 1791, stands on a square in Philadelphia, Pennsylvania.

Based on these early successes as secretary of the treasury, Hamilton grew in power and influence. He helped create the U. S. Coast Guard and the U. S. Navy. He also proposed a naval academy that would train officers. To raise money to support the Army and the Navy, he created a new set of taxes on sugar, tobacco, carriages, and other goods.

Hamilton's taxes were unpopular. After all, the American Revolution had started as a protest against taxes imposed by the British. So Hamilton wasn't surprised when Pennsylvania farmers reacted violently to the tax on whiskey.

In September 1791, a tax collector in western Pennsylvania was tarred and feathered by those opposed to the whiskey tax. When a federal agent was sent to summon those who had committed the crime to court, he was tarred and feathered, too.

The violence didn't change Hamilton's mind about taxes, but he did suggest a few changes to the whiskey tax to calm the situation. He increased duties paid on alcohol imported into the United States from other countries, and he decreased taxes

> *In Hamilton's day, tarring and feathering someone was a way of publicly punishing them so they would leave town. People smeared hot, sticky tar on the victim and then covered him with feathers. Tar was easy to find where ships were built, and feathers were plentiful. This was an extremely cruel practice and caused the victim great pain and humiliation.*

paid on alcohol made within the country. This helped American alcohol producers make a bit more money. Hamilton, however, stood firm in his belief that the new nation must collect taxes. He told President Washington that it was important for the federal government to show that its laws must be followed.

Between the fall of 1792 and the spring of 1794, the controversery raged. The Treasury Department and the defiant farmers came to a fragile truce, but then more violence occurred. People who opposed the tax threatened the Treasury Department officials and damaged the property of farmers who

Protestors parade a tarred and feathered tax collector in the streets.

paid the tax.

In July 1794, a U.S. marshal, authorized to enforce federal laws, was sent to western Pennsylvania to deliver writs, or search warrants, to farmers who refused to pay their taxes. The marshal made most of his deliveries without incident, but when he got to William Miller's farm, someone fired

Armed citizens captured tax collectors during the Whiskey Rebellion of 1794.

a gun. A few days later, armed protesters set fire to the home of the area's chief tax collector.

As word of the violence spread, opponents of the whiskey tax grew bolder. President Washington asked his Cabinet what he should do. Hamilton and two other Cabinet members urged the president to use military force to end the rebellion. Washington followed their advice.

Despite the fact that his presence would only anger tax opponents more, Hamilton rode with an army of about 15,000 troops to put down the so-called "Whiskey Rebellion" in late September 1794. There was no armed resistance to the troops, but the military had made Washington's point. Hamilton showed he was determined to uphold the federal government's laws.

Although Washington was content with the outcome of the effort, Hamilton was not. Hamilton insisted that leaders of the rebellion should be brought to justice, and he convinced Washington that they should be arrested. "I hope there will be found characters fit for examples

> *Believing his presence alone might end the Whiskey Rebellion, President Washington gathered the militia together himself. Leaving from Philadelphia, he joined the troops gathering along the way before their final stop in Bedford in western Pennsylvania. Once all the troops were assembled, Washington headed back to Philadelphia.*

and who can be made so," Hamilton said to the president.

By the middle of November, about 150 people had been jailed and were awaiting trial in Pittsburgh, Pennsylvania. Meanwhile, the troops—and Hamilton—returned home.

To some Americans, Hamilton was a hero. Others saw him as dangerous. Some people gave Hamilton credit for rescuing the United States from a potential collapse. But some newspapers harshly criticized him for trying to create a federal government with dangerous powers.

The debate on Hamilton's proposals and actions led to the creation of the first American political parties. Hamilton was recognized as the leader of the Federalist Party, which stood for a strong federal government funded by taxes. The party also wanted the United States to be allied with Great Britain. Their opposition, the Democratic-Republican Party led by Thomas Jefferson, wanted individual states to have a greater say in government. They also

Though he disagreed with Hamilton's economic plans for the country, James Madison did favor a strong federal government. At the Constitutional Convention, Madison helped design the checks and balances among the three branches of government—the executive, judicial, and legislative. Because of his hard work during the convention, he is sometimes called "the father of the Constitution."

wanted to be allied with France instead of Britain.

As Hamilton's influence grew, he seemed to make more and more enemies. Two powerful enemies were James Madison and Thomas Jefferson, a fellow Cabinet member. Both men worked to defeat his economic plans for the United States. They believed that Hamilton was corrupt, and Jefferson even wrote a letter to President Washington saying so.

Thomas Jefferson (1743-1826) served as the 3rd president of the United States from 1801-1809.

In the letter, Jefferson claimed Hamilton hoped to get rid of the U.S. Constitution and overthrow the government. He said that Hamilton's goal was "a change from the present republican form of government to that of a monarchy, of which the English Constitution is to be the model." Washington answered that the charges against Hamilton were ridiculous. It wouldn't be long before Jefferson resigned as secretary of state.

Behind the scenes, Jefferson and Madison continued working to remove Hamilton as secretary of the treasury. They were helped by Congressman

Statue of Hamilton in front of the Treasury Department building in Washington, D.C.

William B. Giles of Virginia.

On January 23, 1793, Giles accused Hamilton of handling the public debt in ways that weren't legal. He said Hamilton used money borrowed to pay the foreign debt to pay interest charges on domestic debt instead. Giles pointed out that Congress had not given Hamilton the authority to move money around that way.

Along with supervising his staff at the Department of the Treasury, one of Hamilton's primary duties was to prepare long reports on the department's activities. Giles said he believed Hamilton gave Congress misleading reports and at times failed to report activity from the Department of the Treasury at all. Giles also claimed that Hamilton couldn't account for about $1.5 million in government funds. He even hinted that the secretary of the treasury had stolen them.

Outraged, Hamilton immediately went to work to disprove the charges and to clear his name. In less than a month, Hamilton and his staff wrote a history of the Department of the Treasury's business since it was created. Hamilton flooded Congress with long reports, including documents and statistics to prove the reports were honest. In a landslide vote, Congress cleared Hamilton of any wrongdoing.

Hamilton's strong beliefs and his willingness to share them openly gave his enemies many reasons to want to destroy his character. Even in his home state of New York, Hamilton had bitter rivals. One of them was a state senator named Aaron Burr.

Burr and Hamilton both were young, ambitious lawyers. They took opposing sides in several different election campaigns, however, and soon grew to dislike each other intensely. Their rivalry would prove to have disastrous results. ❧

9 FINAL YEARS

Chapter

❧❦❧

In the late summer of 1793, a yellow fever epidemic ravaged Philadelphia, taking thousands of lives. Alexander Hamilton became ill on September 6. It appeared he would not recover.

When Dr. Edward Stevens heard that Hamilton was ill, he came to his bedside. Stevens, Hamilton's good friend from his early days in the West Indies, was the son of the man who gave Hamilton a home after his mother died. Stevens successfully treated Hamilton's fever.

Within a week, Hamilton felt better, although he remained weak. His wife Elizabeth had been struck by the disease, too, but she was also recovering. Once they felt up to it, Hamilton and his wife traveled to Elizabeth's family home, the Schuyler man-

The Schuyler Mansion, built in 1762, stands in Albany, New York.

sion in Albany, New York, to continue their recoveries. They wanted to see their children, who had gone to stay with Grandma and Grandpa Schuyler to avoid the epidemic.

Their trip to Albany wasn't easy. When they reached the outskirts of Albany on September 21, the Hamiltons were told they couldn't enter the city. The mayor and town council had decided that travelers from Philadelphia wouldn't be allowed to visit until the yellow fever outbreak was over. They were afraid the yellow fever would spread to Albany.

When Albany town leaders discovered these travelers weren't ordinary Philadelphia citizens, they loosened their restrictions a bit. Town doctors were called to check on the couple's health. When the doctors declared the visitors disease-free, the city council allowed the Hamiltons to enter Albany, despite the outrage of some community residents. The mayor of Albany described the situation:

> *The fears of the citizens [are] beyond conception, from the idea that the carriages and baggage of . . . Hamilton and servants may contain infection and possibly spread the disorder.*

Although the mayor believed the fears of the citizens were unfounded, the council remained cautious. The Hamiltons were forced to destroy their clothing, leave their luggage behind, and travel in the open air without servants. They could go to the Schuyler mansion only, where they would be quarantined, or isolated from all other people. Hamilton was angry, but he was too tired and weak to put up an argument. For once, Hamilton just said nothing.

The Hamiltons stayed with the Schuylers into the month of October before returning to Philadelphia. For a month after their return, Hamilton was occasionally ill. Even so, he managed to catch up on the business of the Department of the Treasury and attend Cabinet meetings.

Within a year, Hamilton was considering retiring from public service. On December 1, 1794, he told President Washington and the speaker of the House of Representatives that he planned to resign from public office on January 31.

He decided that now was the time to step away from public service and concentrate on his family. After helping the new nation with its finances, Hamilton hoped to make more money in order to better support his growing family, which would eventually include eight children. "Having contributed to place [the finances] of the nation on good footing, I go to take a little care of my own: which need my care not a little," Hamilton wrote to a family member.

At the Department of the Treasury, Hamilton worked on the paperwork that had stacked up while he was fighting the Whiskey Rebellion. He also readied his department staff to work without him.

As planned, he retired from the Department of the Treasury at the end of January 1795. In mid-February, the Hamilton family left Philadelphia for a long vacation. First, they stopped in New York City, where Hamilton was honored at a banquet attended by more than 200 of the city's leading residents.

A statue of Alexander Hamilton stands in front of his home in New York City.

In early March, the Hamiltons arrived at the Schuyler mansion. They stayed with Elizabeth's family for about three months and then returned to their home at 63 Pine St. in New York City. In addition to being the family home, the Pine Street location also became the office of Hamilton's law practice. The family truly would spend more time together, whether Hamilton was working or not.

With the name he had made for himself during his government service, Hamilton's law practice thrived. Though the fees he charged were low, he still managed to make three to four times more than the $3,000 he had made each year as secretary of the treasury.

In 1797, Hamilton's political enemies again accused him of having illegally profited from his job as secretary of the treasury. While Hamilton denied that he had broken any laws, he did admit to some wrongdoing in his life. He said he had had an extramarital affair with a woman named Maria Reynolds. This public confession made him the target of jokes and attacks on his character. Embarrassed and ashamed, Hamilton asked for—and received—Elizabeth's forgiveness.

Even though he still had many enemies in government, including the current president, John Adams, Hamilton returned to public service in July 1798. With American involvement in the French Revolution a possibility, George Washington strongly suggested that President Adams name Hamilton as inspector general of the U.S. Army. Despite his dislike for Hamilton, Adams knew better than to go against Washington, one of the most popular men in the country.

The French Revolution lasted from 1789 to 1799. It reformed the French government and ended the supreme rule of French kings. Other European monarchs feared the spread of democratic ideas. U.S. leaders were torn about whether the United States should be drawn into the bloody conflict, but the French Revolution and France's war with Great Britain ended without U.S. participation.

Hamilton had always liked being involved with the military, and he jumped at the chance to build a strong army for his country. Though he would serve as inspector general until June 2, 1800, he never really got the chance to do much good.

As president of the United States, John Adams purposely made Hamilton's job difficult. Because he didn't trust Hamilton, Adams didn't want to see him succeed in building a strong, new army and make himself more powerful. Adams also wanted the United States to remain neutral in the French Revolution and France's war with Great Britain. Perhaps he feared a strong military would make it easier for the United States to go to war.

As inspector general, Hamilton discovered that military supplies and equipment were scarce. Officers had to be hired before enlistment of soldiers could proceed. President Adams delayed the appointment of officers so long that Hamilton couldn't begin recruiting soldiers. When the French

John Adams, who had been Washington's vice president, was elected the country's second president and held that office from 1797 to 1801.

Revolution ended and war with France was no longer a danger, Adams ended enlistment in the new army and then disbanded it altogether. Hamilton's service as inspector general proved to be the most frustrating time in his entire public life.

After he returned to private life, Alexander continued to play an active part in politics, and he continued to anger his enemies. In the presidential election of 1800, Federalist candidate John Adams sought to be reelected. He chose as his running mate Charles C. Pinckney of South Carolina. The Democratic-Republicans chose Thomas Jefferson as their presidential candidate and Aaron Burr as the vice presidential candidate.

Aaron Burr served as vice president of the United States under Thomas Jefferson.

Hamilton then caused a split in the Federalist Party by suggesting Pinckney be chosen as the country's next president instead of Adams. He wrote a long attack on Adams, which he meant only a few people to see. When the letter fell into Burr's hands, the Democratic-Republican showed it to as many people as he could in order to make the Federalists look bad.

Adams was defeated in the presidential race by an electoral vote of 73 to 65. But there was a problem. At this time, the candidate who received the second-highest number of electoral votes—no matter what party he belonged to—won the vice presidency.

Each Democratic-Republican had cast one vote for Jefferson and one vote for Burr. By their votes, the electors intended to choose Jefferson for the presidency and Burr for the vice presidency. However, technically, both men were tied in the vote for the office of president.

Burr could have cleared up the mess by withdrawing from

Charles C. Pinckney (1746-1825) was born in Charleston, South Carolina, but received most of his education in England. A lawyer who embraced the patriot cause, Pinckney was one of the leaders at the Constitutional Convention. He was present at every session and argued in favor of a powerful national government. Pinckney proposed that senators should serve without pay, and urged that slaves be counted equally with whites in determining representation.

the presidential race and becoming vice president, as the electors had intended. Instead, realizing he had a chance to become president, he remained silent. Therefore, the election went to the House of Representatives to decide.

Hamilton gave his support to his old enemy Thomas Jefferson instead of Burr. Though Hamilton

The view down Pennsylvania Avenue from Capitol Hill in Washington, D.C., in 1800

didn't like either man, he saw Jefferson as the lesser of two evils. "Jefferson is to be preferred," Hamilton wrote to Oliver Wolcott Jr., who succeeded him as secretary of the treasury. "He is by far not so dangerous a man and he has pretensions [claims] to character." As for Burr, Hamilton wrote, "There is nothing in his favor." Hamilton believed that Burr only sought personal glory, power, and wealth.

The vote in the House of Representatives

between Burr and Jefferson was close. After 36 rounds of balloting, on February 17, 1801, Thomas Jefferson was named the country's third president. Aaron Burr would become the vice president. On March 4, Jefferson went to the unfinished capital city on the Potomac and took the oath of office. Hamilton's very public opinions about the 1800 presidential election would cost him a high personal price in the near future.

In 1801, Hamilton bought a 32-acre (13-hectare)

Thomas Jefferson (1743-1826) was the third president of the United States from 1801-1809.

country estate in New York. With the help of architect John McComb Jr., he designed a two-story house he called the Grange, named after his father's home in Scotland. Although it wasn't quite finished, the Grange became home for the Hamilton family in August 1802. Hamilton, his wife, and their seven children moved into the new house, but the day was bittersweet for Hamilton. He deeply missed his oldest and favorite child, Philip, and wished he was there to enjoy their new home.

Less than a year before, on November 20, 1801, Philip Hamilton had gone with a friend named Price to Park Theater in New York City. Sitting in the next box was George Eacker, a lawyer and supporter of Thomas Jefferson. Eacker had delivered a speech four months earlier that criticized the Federalists, including Alexander Hamilton. Philip and his friend began making fun of Eacker, who told them to meet him in the lobby. When they did, Eacker challenged them both to gun duels. They accepted the challenges.

Days later, Price met Eacker in the first duel. Neither was hurt. Later in the week, Philip and Eacker met for their duel at Powles Hook, New Jersey. Before Philip could fire his pistol, Eacker took aim, shot, and fatally wounded him. When Alexander Hamilton heard the news, he rushed to his son's bedside. Philip, 19, died the next day.

Hamilton was crushed by his son's death and called him "the brightest hope of my family."

After Philip's death, Hamilton had thrown himself into his work and the completion of his new home in New York. He also continued to be outspoken in his political opinions, especially in the case of Aaron Burr.

After working to prevent Burr's election as president in 1800, Hamilton also helped defeat Burr in the race for governor of New York in 1804. He told his friends that Burr could not be trusted with public

A gun duel was a common way to settle a gentlemen's disagreement.

Although dueling was illegal in some states, some people considered it the "gentleman's way" of settling disputes. People who participated in a duel agreed to fight by an elaborate set of rules and to act honorably. Still, anyone who fought a duel ran the real risk of injury or death.

office. "He has no principle, public or private," Hamilton said. He further described Burr as "a man of irregular and unsatiable ambition ... who ought not to be trusted with the reigns of government."

Burr blamed Hamilton for his defeat in the 1804 election. When he learned of Hamilton's harsh words, he demanded that Hamilton apologize. Hamilton refused, and Burr challenged him to a duel.

Several times in his life, Hamilton had challenged other people to duels, but in every case the dispute was settled before the duel was fought. This time would be different.

The two men agreed to meet at Weehawken, New Jersey, on the morning of July 11, 1804. In the days before the duel with Burr, Hamilton went on with his daily life, continuing to work at his law office. He showed few signs of worry about the upcoming duel, yet he did prepare his will and write letters to his wife. Hamilton told her that he would not fire his dueling pistol at Burr. Hamilton explained that he would rather risk his life than take another life in a duel.

The morning of the duel, Hamilton rowed across

the Hudson River from New York to Weehawken with his friend Nathaniel Pendleton and his doctor David Hosack. Burr was waiting for him there.

Burr and Hamilton stood 10 paces apart with pistols loaded. One of the bystanders gave the command to fire. Taking aim, Burr fired at Hamilton first. As Hamilton fell to the ground, his finger involuntarily pulled the trigger of his gun, and a shot went into the air. Burr was unharmed, but Hamilton wasn't as lucky.

Hamilton's friend and doctor, David Hosack, watched as Hamilton and Burr prepared to duel.

The pistols used in the duel fought between Alexander Hamilton and Aaron Burr

Dr. Hosack later told others what happened:

> *I found him half sitting on the ground, supported in the arms of Mr. Pendleton. His countenance of death I shall never forget. He had at that instant just strength to say, 'This is a mortal wound Doctor'; when he sunk away, and became to all appearances lifeless.*

Still, Hamilton clung to life. Pendleton and

Hosack rowed him back to a friend's house in New York City. Burr's bullet had ripped through Hamilton's liver and lodged in his spine. Elizabeth rushed to be with him, and although he was suffering great pain, Hamilton was able to say good-bye. He died quietly at age 49 on the afternoon of July 12, 1804, with his wife at his side.

After Alexander Hamilton's death, Elizabeth Hamilton lived for another 50 years and dedicated herself to charitable causes. For the rest of her life, she wore black in memory of her husband. Elizabeth also worked to preserve her husband's letters and papers as well as his reputation. She died in 1854 at the age of 97.

Alexander Hamilton's contribution as a founding father of the country has been remembered by the people of the United States. The $10 bill, which displays a portrait of Alexander Hamilton, serves as a memorial to his life—a fitting tribute to the first secretary of the treasury and the man who worked to build a firm financial foundation for the United States of America.

> *At the time of his death, Alexander Hamilton likely owed more money than he was worth. His friend Brockholst Livingston said Hamilton's personal finances "had been greatly injured, if not entirely ruined by that gentleman's attention to public business." Hamilton always wanted to provide well for his family, but he never had a goal of becoming wealthy.*

HAMILTON'S LIFE

1772

Leaves West Indies to begin education in Great Britain's American colonies

1755

Born January 11 on the island of Nevis in the West Indies

1750

1759

The British Museum opens in London

1764

James Hargreaves creates the spinning jenny, a mechanical spinning wheel

WORLD EVENTS

1774

Enrolls in King's
College in New
York City

1776

Becomes an artillery
officer in the
Continental Army

1775

1774

King Louis XV of
France dies and his
grandson, Louis XVI
is crowned

1775

The first British
yacht club, the Royal
Thames Yacht Club,
is founded

HAMILTON'S LIFE

1777

Joins the staff of
General George
Washington

1780

Marries Elizabeth
Schuyler December 14

1780

1779

Jan Ingenhousz of the
Netherlands discovers
that plants release
oxygen when exposed
to sunlight

WORLD EVENTS

1787

Attends the
Constitutional
Convention and
writes articles in
support of ratifying
the Constitution

1789

Becomes the first
U.S. secretary of the
treasury

1783

The first manned
hot air balloon flight
is made in Paris,
France, by the
Montgolfier brothers

1789

The French
Revolution begins
with the storming
of the Bastille
prison in Paris

HAMILTON'S LIFE

1791

President George
Washington signs a
law creating a national
bank, as suggested by
Hamilton

1795

Resigns as secretary
of the treasury to
concentrate on
law practice

1790

1795

1795

J. F. Blumenbach
writes his book *The
Human Species* thus
laying the foundation
of anthropology

1793

Poland is divided
between Russia
and Prussia

WORLD EVENTS

1804

Dies after being wounded in a duel with Aaron Burr

1801

Ultraviolet radiation is discovered

1805

General anesthesia is first used in surgery

DATE OF BIRTH: January 11, 1755

BIRTHPLACE: Nevis, an island in the
West Indies

FATHER: James Hamilton
(1718?-1799)

MOTHER: Rachel Fawcett Lavien
(1729?-1768)

EDUCATION: King's College, now
Columbia University,
New York, NY

SPOUSE: Elizabeth Schuyler
(1757-1854)

MARRIED: December 14, 1780

CHILDREN: Philip (1782-1801)
Angelica (1784-1857)
Alexander (1786-?)
James (1788-?)
John (1792-?)
William (1797-1850)
Eliza (1799-?)
Philip (1802-?)

DATE OF DEATH: July 12, 1804

BURIED: Trinity Churchyard,
New York, NY

In the Library

Cunningham, Noble E. Jr. *Jefferson vs. Hamilton: Confrontatioins That Shaped a Nation.* New York: Palgrave Macmillan, 2000.

Ingram, W. Scott. *Aaron Burr and the Young Nation.* Farmington Hills, Mich.: Blackbirch Press, 2002.

Kallen, Stuart A. *Alexander Hamilton.* Edina, Minn.: Abdo and Daughters Publishing, 2001.

Prolman, Marilyn. *The Constitution.* Chicago: Children's Press, 1995.

Rosenburg, John. *Alexander Hamilton.* Brookfield, Conn.: Twenty-first Century Books, 2000.

WEB SITES

For more information on *Alexander Hamilton*, use FactHound to track down Web sites related to this book.

1. Go to *www.facthound.com*
2. Type in a search word related to this book or this book ID.0756508274
3. Click on the *Fetch It* button.

FactHound will find the best Web sites for you.

HISTORIC SITES

Hamilton Grange National Historic Site
287 Convent Ave.
New York, NY 10005
To tour Alexander Hamilton's home

Trinity Churchyard
Broadway and Wall Streets
New York, NY 10006
To visit the final resting place of
Alexander Hamilton

abolish
to put an end to something officially; to ban

aide (short for aide-de-camp)
a military officer acting as assistant to a superior officer

ally
country that supports another country in a conflict

Anti-Federalist
a member of the group opposed to the adoption of the U.S. Constitution and against a strong federal, or central, government

Articles of Confederation
the first constitution of the United States; it gave the central government much less power than the present U.S. Constitution

artillery
large guns, such as cannons

battalion
a large military unit made up of a headquarters and two or more companies of soldiers

bayonet
a blade attached to the end of a rifle and used as a weapon in close combat

deserting
leaving a post in the military without permission

epidemic
a severe outbreak of an infectious, often fatal, disease

Federalist
a member of the group that supported the adoption of the U.S. Constitution and favored a strong federal, or central, government

Glossary

loyalists
Americans who remained loyal to the king of England and supported the British government's policies during the American Revolution

militia
a loosely organized military force, often made up of local volunteers

monarchy
a type of government in which a king or queen is the head of state

radical
someone who believes in extreme political change

ratification
official approval of a law or document

unanimous
agreed on by everyone

veto
to reject or refuse to approve a proposed law

yellow fever
a serious infectious disease caused by a virus carried by the yellow-fever mosquito

Chapter 1

Page 10, line 5: Richard Brookhiser. *Alexander Hamilton: American.* New York: Free Press, 1993, p. 102.

Chapter 2

Page 21, line 1: Alexander Hamilton. *Writings.* New York: Literary Classics of the United States, Inc., 2001, p. 6.

Chapter 4

Page 30, line 23: *Alexander Hamilton: American.*

Page 33, line 21: Stanley Elkins and Eric McKitrick. *The Age of Federalism.* New York: Oxford University Press, p. 54.

Chapter 5

Page 43, line 4: *Writings*, p. 119.

Page 44, line 19: Jacob Ernest Cooke. *Alexander Hamilton.* New York: Scribner's, 1982, pp. 29-30.

Page 46, line 2: Alexander Hamilton. "Letters to John Laurens, August 15, 1783." www.alexanderhamiltonexhibition.org/letters.

Chapter 6

Page 57, line 9: *The Age of Federalism.* p. 102.

Chapter 7

Page 63, line 7: *Alexander Hamilton*, p. 153.

Chapter 8

Page 73, line 27: Ibid., p. 132.

Page 75, line 20: Ibid., p. 158.

Chapter 9

Page 81, line 10: Ibid., p. 226.

Page 82, line 13: Alexander Hamilton. "Letter to Gouverneur Morris, December 24, 1800." http://odur.let.rug.nl/~usa/B/hamilton/hamil38.htm.

Page 88, line 2: *Alexander Hamilton.* p. 739.

Page 92, line 1: Ibid., p. 242.

Page 94, line 2: Ibid.

Page 95, sidebar: Ibid., p. 158.

Brookhiser, Richard. *Alexander Hamilton: American*. New York: Free Press, 1999.

Cooke, Jacob Ernest. *Alexander Hamilton: A Profile*. New York: Farrar Straus and Giroux, 1969.

Gordon, John Steele. *Hamilton's Blessing: The Extraordinary Life and Times of Our National Debt*. New York: Walker and Co., 1997.

"Hamilton Grange." *National Park Service*. http://www.nps.gov/hagr/.

McDonald, Forrest. *Alexander Hamilton*. New York: W.W. Norton, 1979.

Mitchell, Broadus. *Alexander Hamilton: Youth to Maturity 1755–1788*. New York: Macmillan, 1957.

Morse Jr., John T. *The Life of Alexander Hamilton*. Boston: Little, Brown, and Co., 1876.

Randall, Willard Sterne. *Alexander Hamilton: A Life*. New York: Harper Collins, 2003.

Rogov, Arnold A. *Hamilton and Burr: A Fatal Friendship*. New York: Hill and Wang, 1998.

Wise, William. *Alexander Hamilton*. An Author's Guild Backinprint.com Edition, 2001. http://corppub.iuniverse.com/marketplace/backin-print/0595187943.html.

Brenda Haugen is the author and editor of many books, most of them for children. A graduate of the University of North Dakota in Grand Forks, Brenda lives in North Dakota with her family.

Image Credits

Bettmann/Corbis, cover (top), 4–5, 28, 39, 66, 93, 98 (top right), 101 (top); Stock Montage/Getty Images, cover (bottom), 2, 42, 55, 64, 89; Library of Congress, 8, 45, 49, 96 (bottom left), 99 (bottom); Mary Evans Picture Library, 10, 96 (top); Tony Roberts/Corbis, 12; The Granger Collection, New York, 15, 94; North Wind Picture Archives, 17, 22, 26, 31, 35, 41, 47, 50, 52, 54, 56, 61, 62, 71, 72, 88, 97, 98 (top left), 99 (top); MPI/Getty Images, 19, 75, 85, 86; Hulton Archive/Getty Images, 24, 91, 96 (bottom right); Time Life Pictures/Mansell/Getty Images, 32; Photospin, 58; Lee Snider/Photo Images/Corbis, 69, 80, 100 (left); Alex Wong/Getty Images, 76, 100 (right); Archivo Iconografico, S.A./Corbis, 78; Ferrell Grehan/Corbis, 83; Image Ideas, 98 (bottom); Photodisc, 101 (bottom).